Sight Read Successfully
BOOK 3

by Louise Guhl

To the Teacher

Sight Read Successfully, Book 3 has forty short, fresh selections carefully designed to provide experience in playing at sight in time. They are organized into eight Sets, one per week.

In this book, students read material designed to help them see notes grouped into patterns and to realize them as shapes in the hand. At the same time, students develop the ability to identify the exact metric location of fingering indications in the score and changes in keyboard locations of patterns. They also learn how to hear and feel the rhythm before playing, thus propelling the fingers to keep the rhythm flowing.

The music to be read has been designed to keep those complexities at a minimum of difficulty so that with good concentration and a judicious tempo pianists can develop the ability to play coherently at sight.

Sight Read Successfully, Book 3 supplements **The Magic Reader, Book 5**, which emphasizes chord reading.

About the Author

Louise Guhl's continuing observation and excitement about how students learn led to the publication of **The Magic Readers, Books 1, 2, 3, 4,** and **5** and **Sight Read Successfully, Books 1, 2,** and **3.** Mrs. Guhl is an independent piano teacher in Dassel, Minnesota, who is also popular as a clinician. In the past she has taught pedagogy and class piano at the University of Minnesota, the MacPhail School of Music, and Concordia College (St. Paul).

After graduation from St. Olaf College she studied in Berlin, Germany. Mrs. Guhl has also been a piano student of Guy Maier and Bernhard Weiser, and a pedagogy student of Guy Duckworth. She is the author of *Keyboard Proficiency* for college students.

ISBN 0-8497-9435-8

©1991 Neil A. Kjos Music Company, 4380 Jutland Drive, San Diego, California 92117. International copyright secured. All rights reserved. Printed in U.S.A.
WARNING! All the music and text in this book are protected by copyright law. To copy or reproduce them by any method is an infringement of the copyright law. Anyone who reproduces copyrighted matter is subject to substantial penalties and assessments for each infringement.

WP322

SET 1

Hearing the Rhythm When You Look At the Notes

At the Lesson

Look at the score (the printed notes) of this piece.

Can you hear how the rhythm of the right hand part goes?

Play the right hand part with rhythmn sticks without counting aloud.

Did it feel good? Did it make sense? If not, point to the notes as you count steadily.

Play it again with rhythm sticks without counting aloud.

When your playing sounds right, "vocalize" the rhythm by using any syllable you like for each note.

It might be like this:

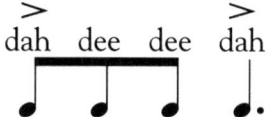  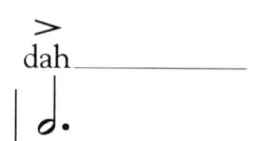

Vocalize it again as you clap the rhythm of the left hand this way.

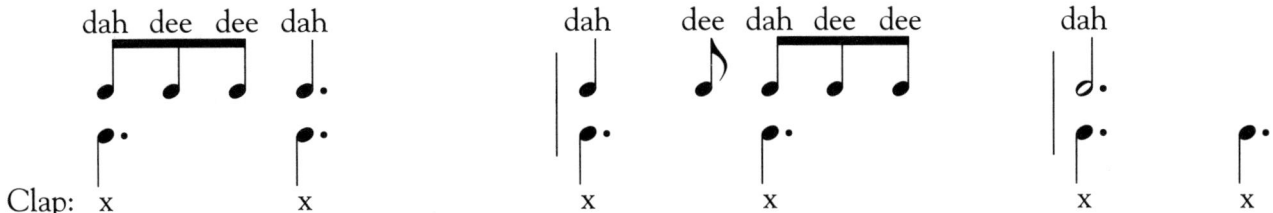

Hearing and feeling the rhythm this way makes it "come alive" even the first time you play a piece.

Before you play the piece do one more thing: notice how often you play three-note patterns of seconds. While playing, try to see each whole pattern in one quick glance, just as you read a whole word in one glance.

If you play a wrong note, do not correct it! Keep going!

After you play the piece, imagine what tempo and shading it should have.

You "shade" your playing when you change the dynamics (loud or soft) as you go along:

Write any dynamic marks you wish in the score.

Play it again. Did you "make music?" Do you think of a title?

Before Your Next Lesson
Each day before you sight read the selection, vocalize the rhythm of the right hand as you clap the part for the left hand.

Scan the score for changes in hand position or irregular fingering.

Play with this goal in mind: to play continuously from beginning to end the first time through. Keep the rhythm, even if you have to leave out some notes!

Then think about the musical sound and decide on tempo and expression marks.

Play it again to make music!

DAY 1

Always try to play the first beat of each measure on time, even if you have to skip some notes to get there.

DAY 2

DAY 3

WP322

SET 2
Crossing the Thumb Under On Time

At the Lesson
Do you have a name for the passages (a succession of notes played without stopping) in these two measures?

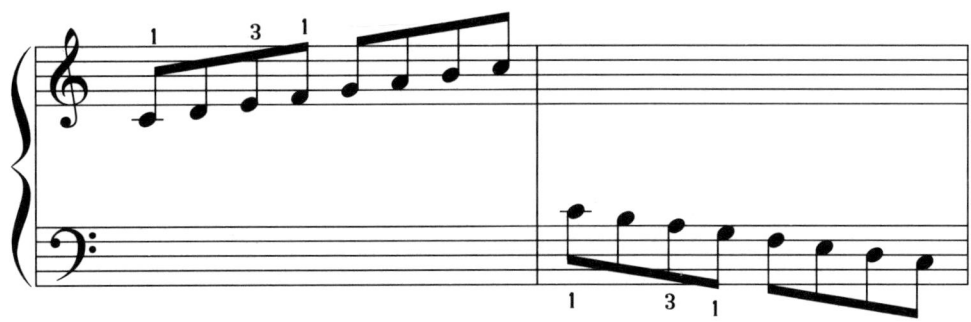

Vocalize the rhythm, accenting the first note of each group printed on a beam. Eighth notes are usually beamed four to a beam. The first note on each beam comes on an accent.

 This is a beam.

Which beats did you accent?

Which finger plays on the third beat?

When does the thumb cross under in order to have that finger ready at the right time?

The grouping helps you see when it is time to make a thumb crossing.

WP322

Before Your Next Lesson

Scan each piece to see if you think you need to vocalize and clap the rhythm.

After playing, decide on tempo and expression.

DAY 3

Check the clef signs!

SET 3

Crossing the Thumb Over On Time

At the Lesson

A passage often starts with the fifth finger, and the thumb playing on an accented note, followed by a crossing finger.

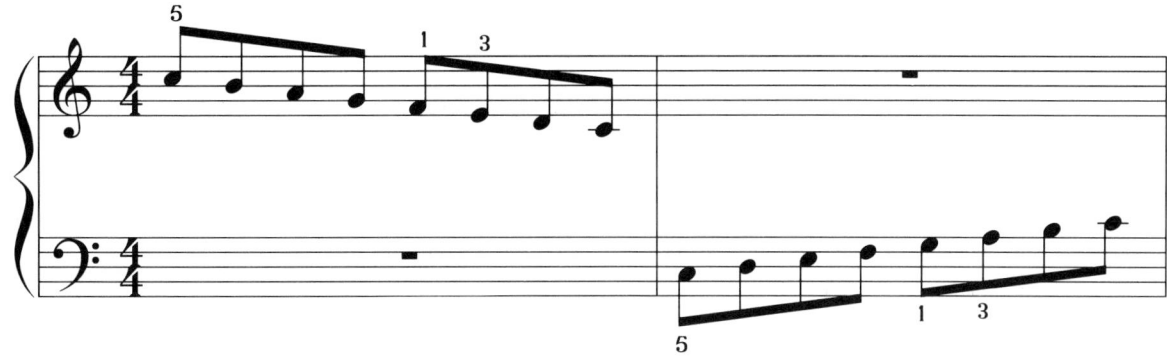

Play this exercise three times without stopping, keeping the rhythm flowing from hand to hand.

Before Your Next Lesson

DAY 1

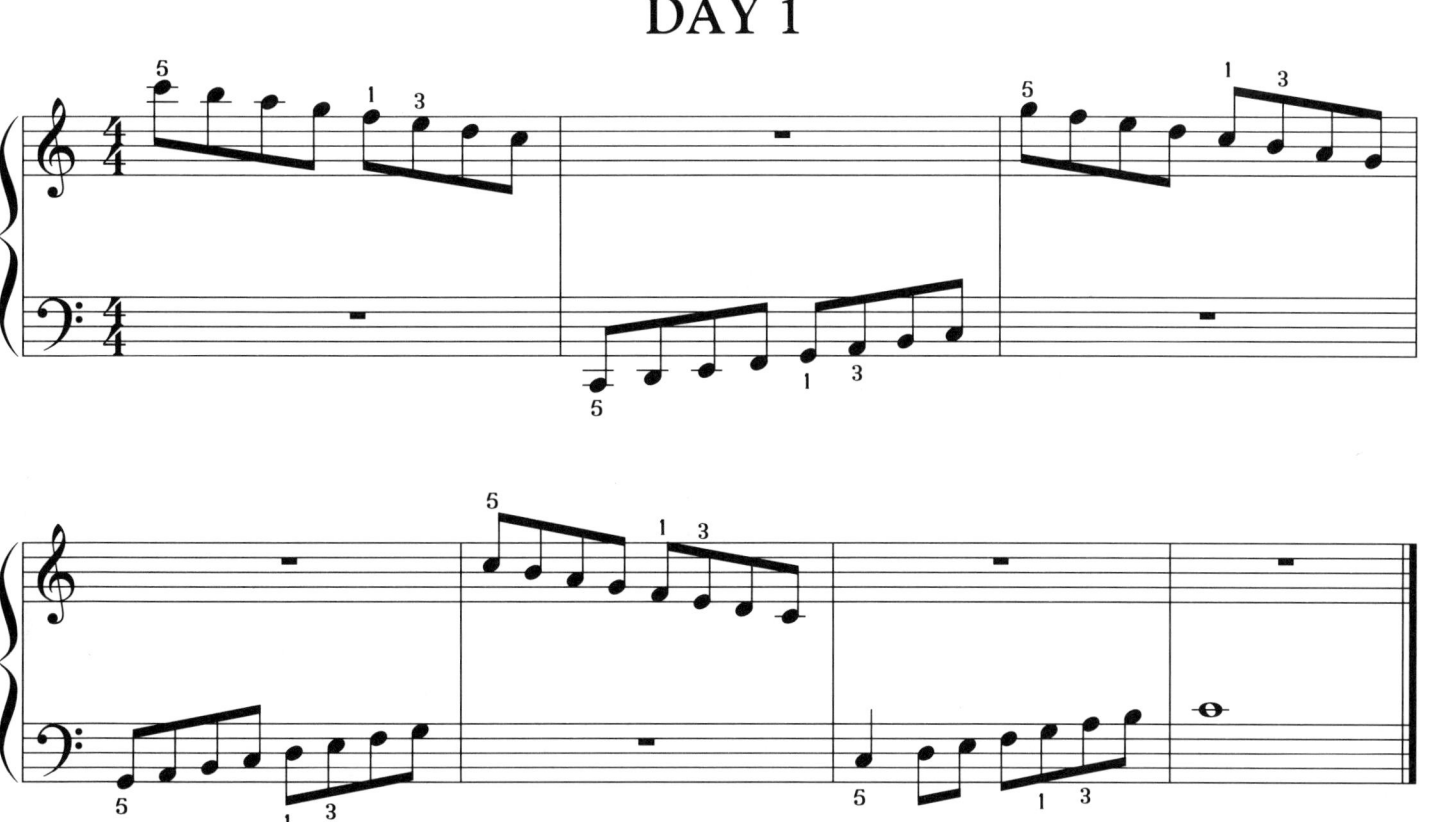

WP322

DAY 2

The change in rhythm places the second finger on the accent.

DAY 3

DAY 4

Be sure to take time to vocalize this, and to feel the keys silently with your fingers to prepare the fingering before you play.

DAY 5

Silently touch left hand fifths before you play.

SET 4

Playing Note Patterns In Time

At the Lesson

Scan this score.

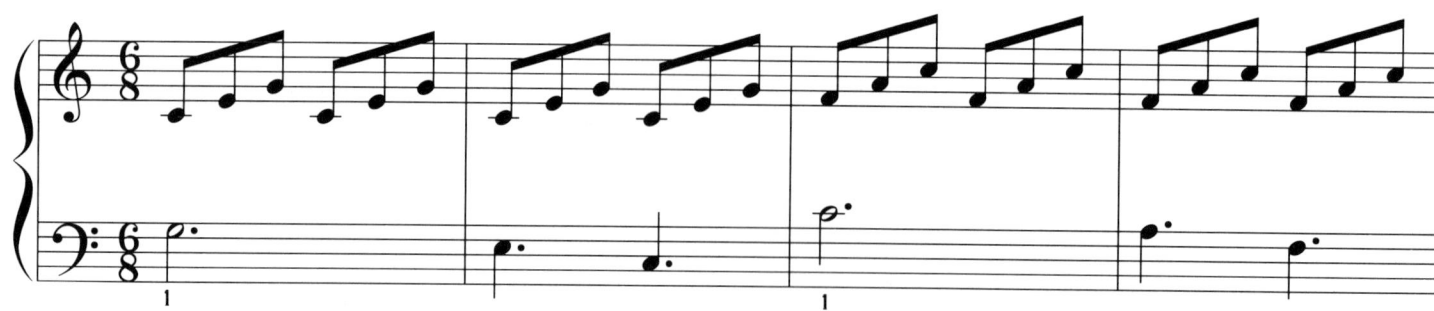

How many notes make a pattern in the right hand?

How many beats does it take to complete the pattern?

How many times is the pattern repeated before it is moved to other keys?

What happens to the pattern during the eight measures of the score?

Is there a pattern in the left hand?

Does it match the right hand pattern in any way?

Play the score, keeping the pattern going like a good motor—well oiled. The fingering should be very clear when you know the pattern!

WP322

Before Your Next Lesson

DAY 1

Look for patterns in both hands before you play.

Try to hear how the music goes in your head as you look at the score.

DAY 2

As you look at the score, feel the fingering.

You will like pedal with this. Try it the first time you play it.

If you do not like the sound, try it again with a different pedaling.

DAY 3

Plan for the clef change in the right hand.

Notice how many measures long the pattern is, and plan for the measures that do not fit the pattern.

Do you need to prepare the hand positions before playing, or can you find them as you go?

DAY 4

The pattern of notes in the left hand never changes. The rhythm pattern is the same until near the end. The measures of rest in the right hand help you change the right hand positions on time.

DAY 5

Be sure you hold the keys down for the tied chords so you can hear the sound as long as they are supposed to last!

SET 5

Seeing First Inversion Chords As Shapes

At the Lesson

Scan this score:

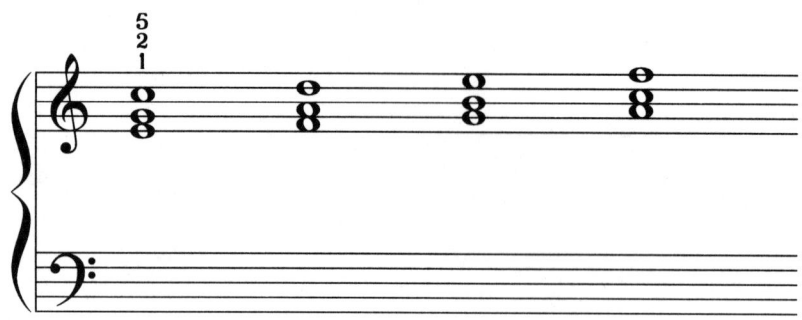

How wide is each chord from the lowest key to the highest?

To play the lowest and highest key together, you must stretch from finger _____ (number) to finger _____.

To play from the lowest key to the middle key you must stretch from finger _____ to _____.

Play this pattern up the keyboard and down one octave, first looking at your hand, then with your eyes closed.

Scan this score for the left hand:

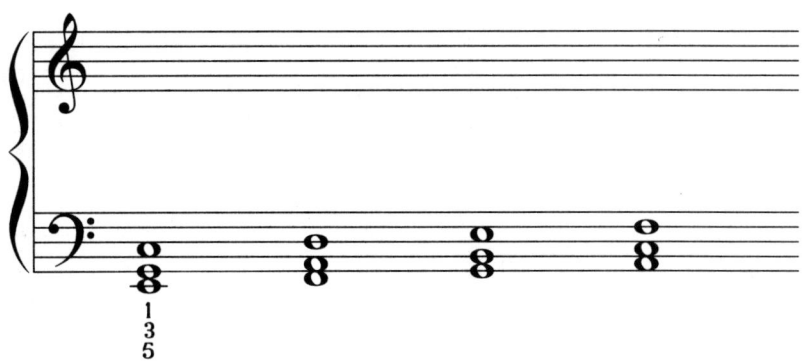

The chords are _____ keys wide.

In each, the middle key is played with a stretch from finger _____ to finger _____ .

Play this pattern up and down one octave, first watching your hand, then with your eyes closed.

Before Your Next Lesson

Each day, look for chord patterns. See the *whole* pattern, not single notes.

When you have seen the pattern and know what keys to play you can pay attention to the other hand, and plan the movement from note to note.

Fingering is given only when the regular chord fingering does not work.

WP322

DAY 1

DAY 2

If you scan for hand positions, perhaps you can pedal as you sight read!

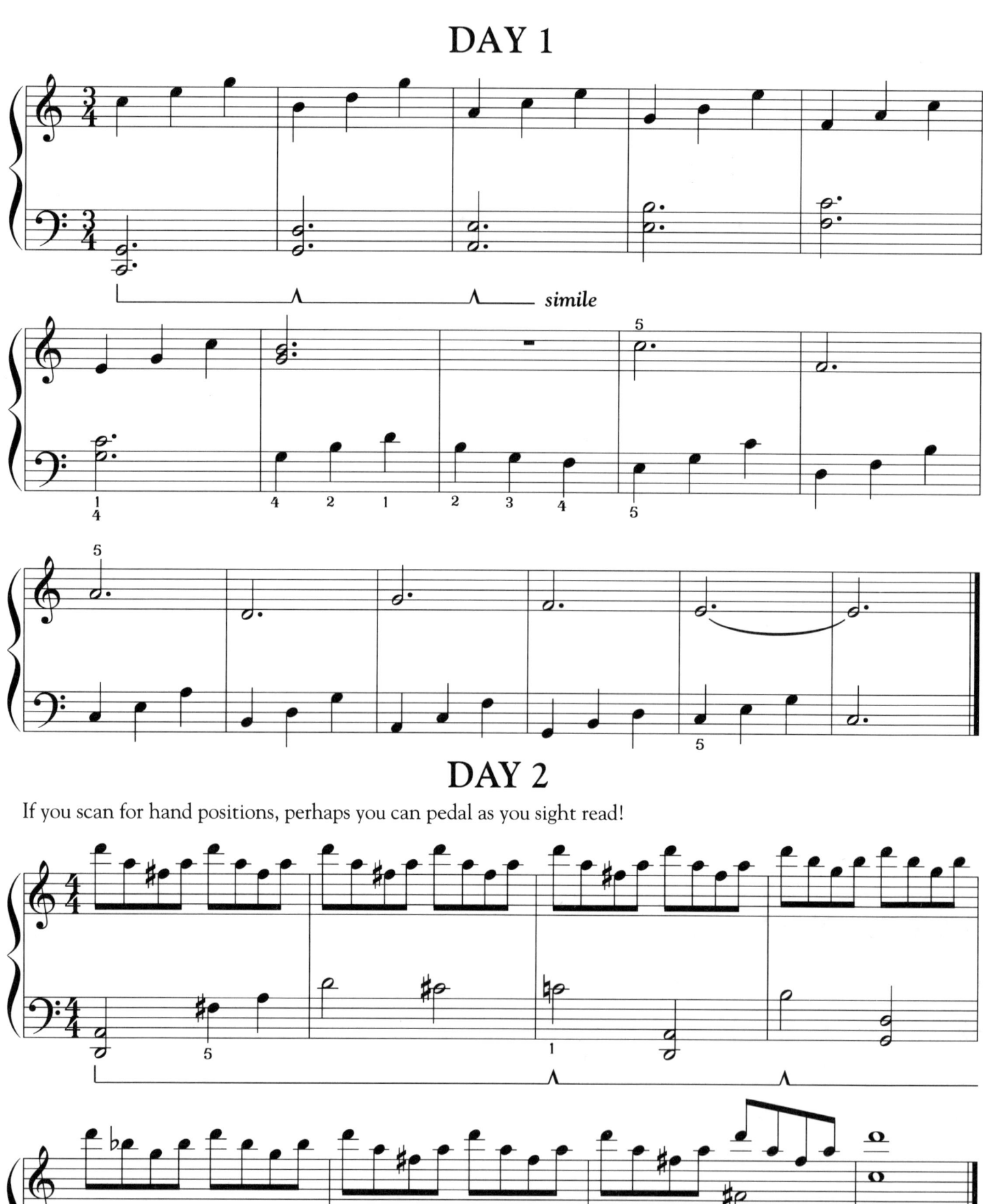

DAY 5

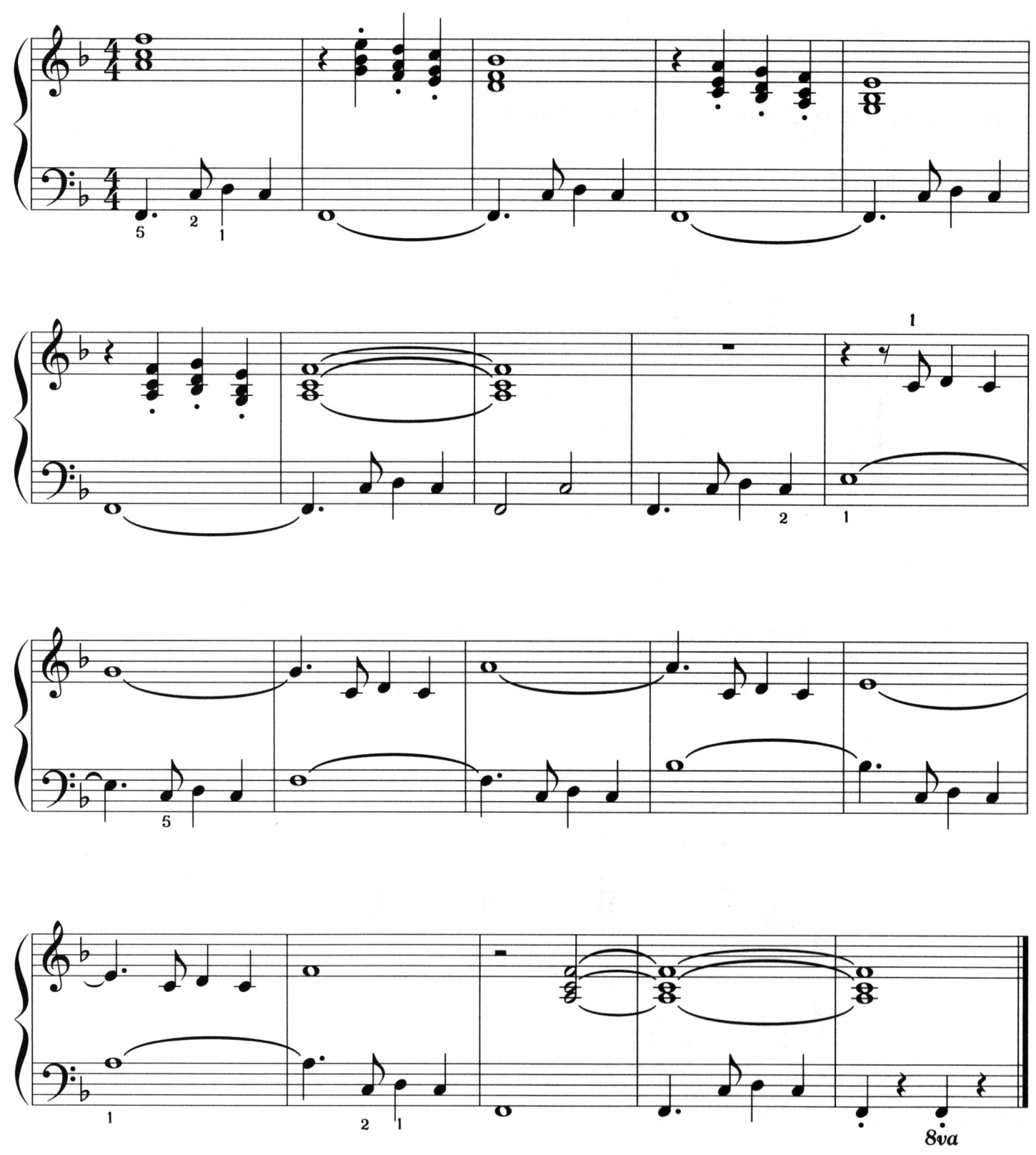

SET 6

Playing Syncopated Rhythms

At the Lesson

With a pencil, write the counting below the notes in this melody. Write "+" only when there is a note to play on "+."

Count aloud and tap the rhythm.

Do the same and tap your foot on the beats.

Beat time with your foot while counting and tapping the rhythm. You may whisper the tied notes if you wish.

Erase each "+."

Tap the rhythm as you count the beats.

Beat time with your foot while you tap the rhythmn of the melody.

Play the melody as you beat time with your foot. Then play it without beating time. Which way did you like better?

Did you recognize this melody? It is from a famous ragtime piece, *The Entertainer,* by Scott Joplin.

How many times did you play a note right after a beat, and then hold it through the next beat? **This is syncopation.**

WP322

Before Your Next Lesson

DAY 1

Tap these rhythms three times without stopping, ending with a whole note.

Count beats only. All are in 4/4 time.

Tap them the same way, but instead of counting, beat time with your foot.

DAY 2

WP322

DAY 3

DAY 4

DAY 5

SET 7

Seeing Second Inversion Chords As Shapes

At the Lesson

Compare the shapes of these chords:

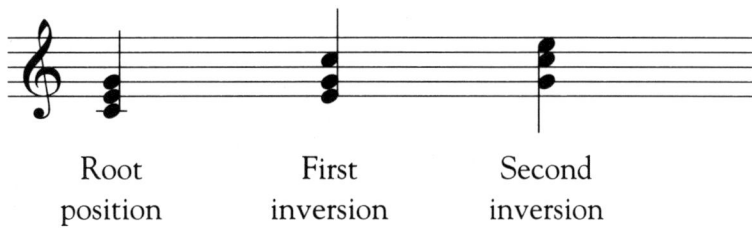

Root position   First inversion   Second inversion

Fill in the blanks:

Root Position
The interval from the lowest note to the highest is a _____ .
The interval from the lowest note to the middle is a _____ .

First Inversion
The interval from the lowest note to the highest is a _____ .
The interval from the lowest note to the middle is a _____ .

Second Inversion
The interval from the lowest note to the highest is a _____ .
The interval from the lowest note to the middle is a _____ .

Compare the fingering:

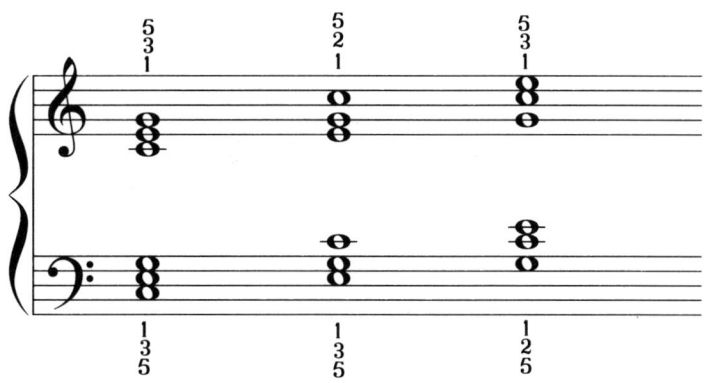

In which position does the right hand play second finger?

In which position does the left hand play second finger?

Play all three positions of F chord correctly fingered.

Play all three positions of G chord correctly fingered.

Before Your Next Lesson

DAY 1

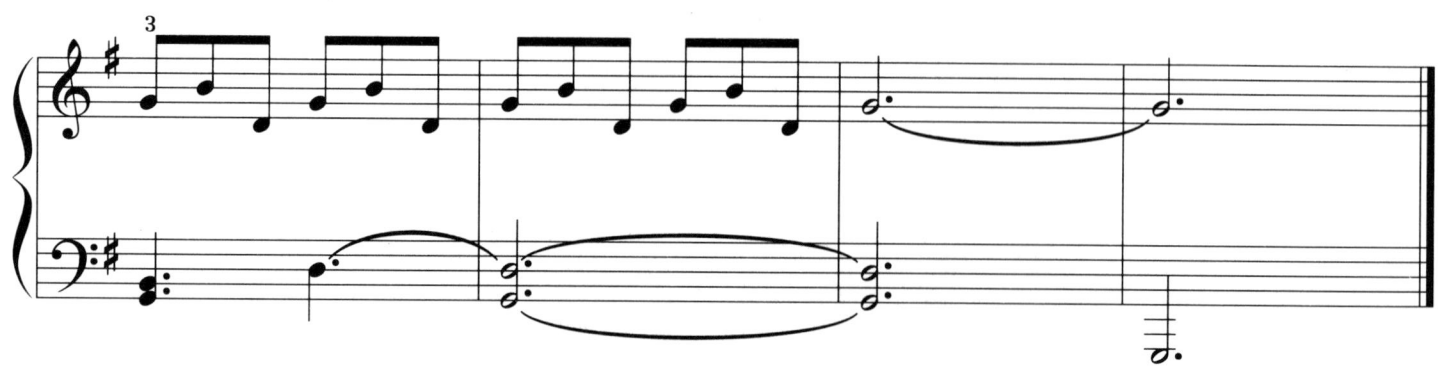

DAY 2

DAY 3

DAY 4

DAY 5

SET 8

Reading Progressions Of Triads and Seventh Chords

At the Lesson

When one chord follows another chord, it makes a chord progression. In this progression, C chord is followed by which chord? _____

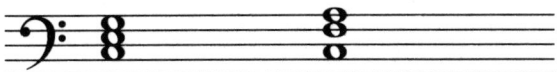

Both the above chords are triads.

Another kind of chord is a seventh chord. It looks like this:

Very often one note is left out because it sounds better.

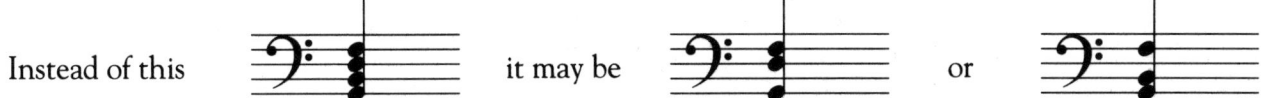

When a seventh chord is inverted, there is always an interval of a second:

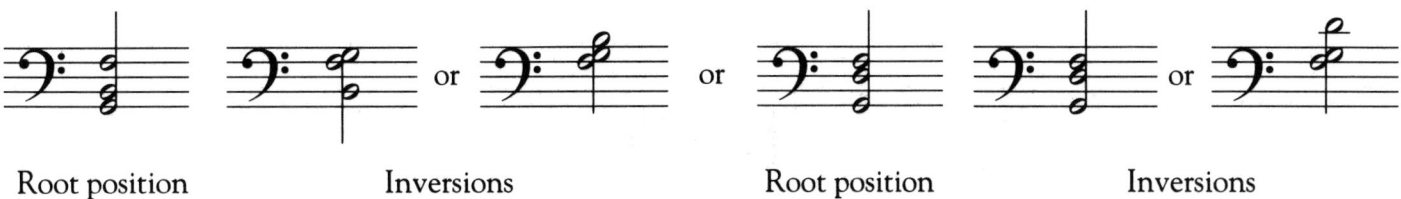

Root position   Inversions   Root position   Inversions

WP322

A seventh chord often comes between two triads:

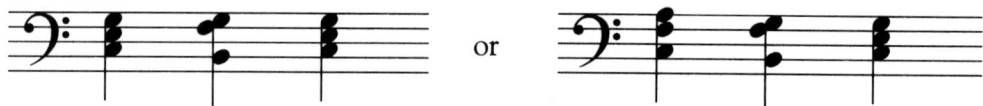

When reading from one chord to the next, think of the bottom, middle and top. These are called "voices" in the chord.

Look at these progressions:

Which voices moved? Which way? Draw lines between the notes to show the movement of voices.

Continue drawing lines in each progression.

The best way to read chord progressions is to feel what your fingers do from one chord to the next.

When you play the first chord, do you already have a finger on a key to be played in the second chord?

Notice that fingers 2 and 4 are on the keys in the second chord.

Do you have to move a finger from one key to another?

Describe what you did.

Do you have to move a finger to a key you just played with another finger?

Describe what you did.

Before Your Next Lesson

DAY 1

Practice all chord progressions on pages 37 and 38 as you

watch your hands, and

with your eyes closed.

Practice them an octave higher with your right hand.

WP322

DAY 2

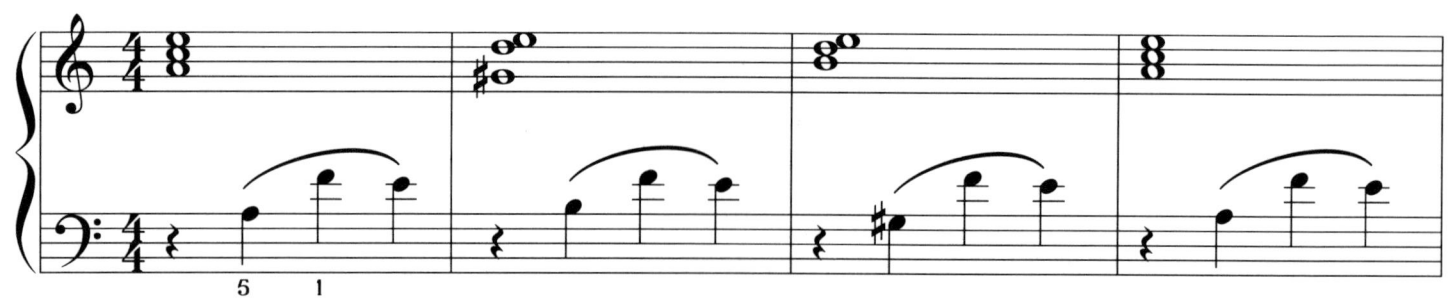

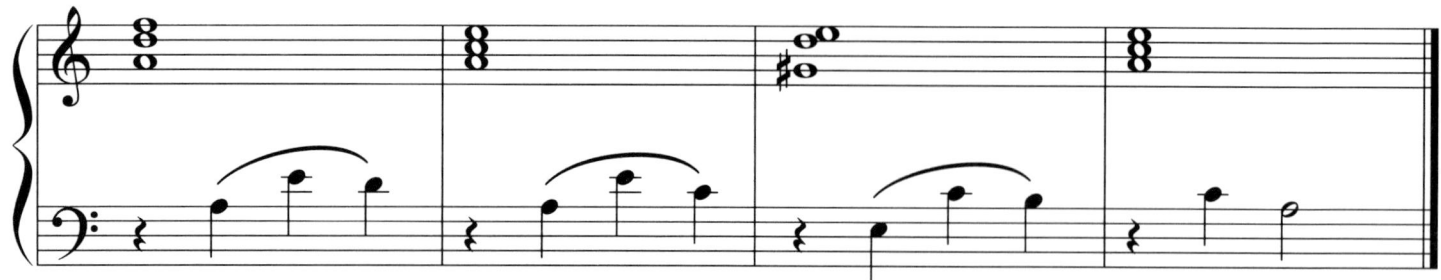

DAY 3

Touch the chords silently before you play. They feel quite different from the chords you have been playing.

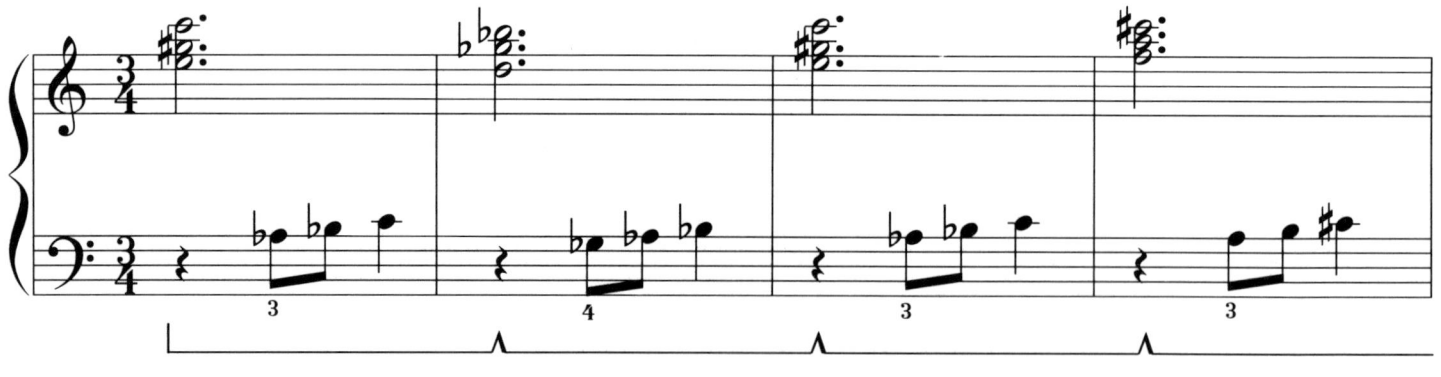

DAY 4

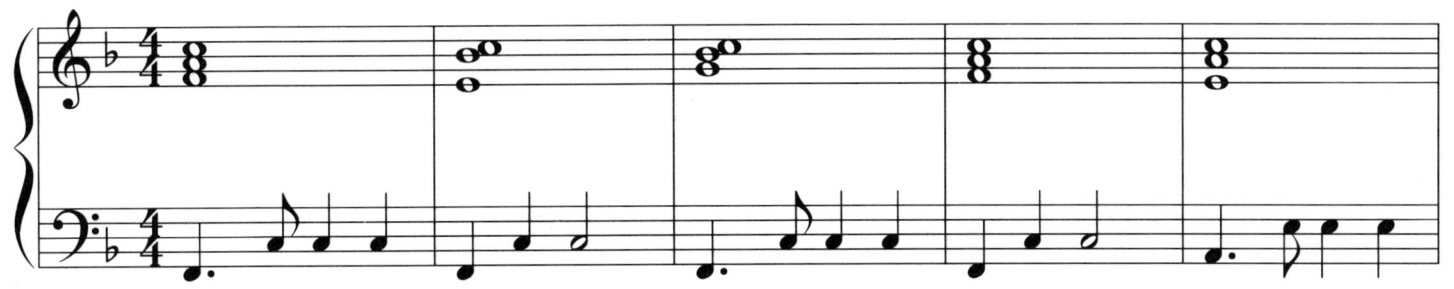
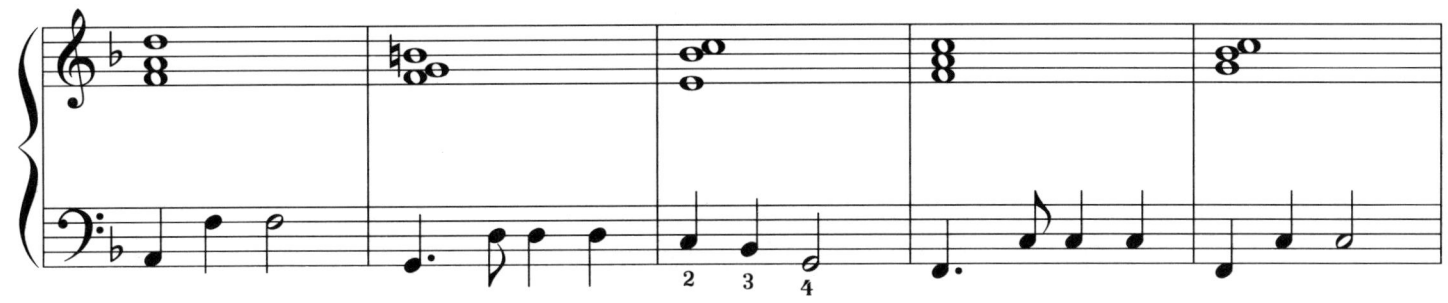
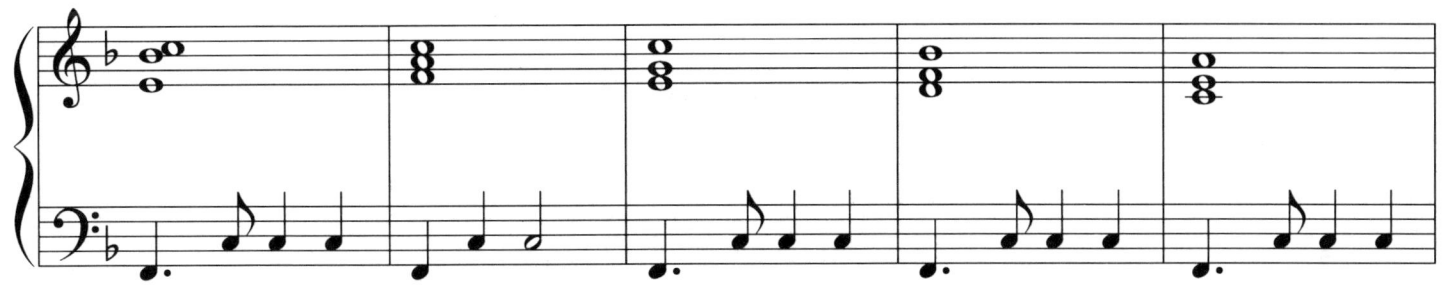
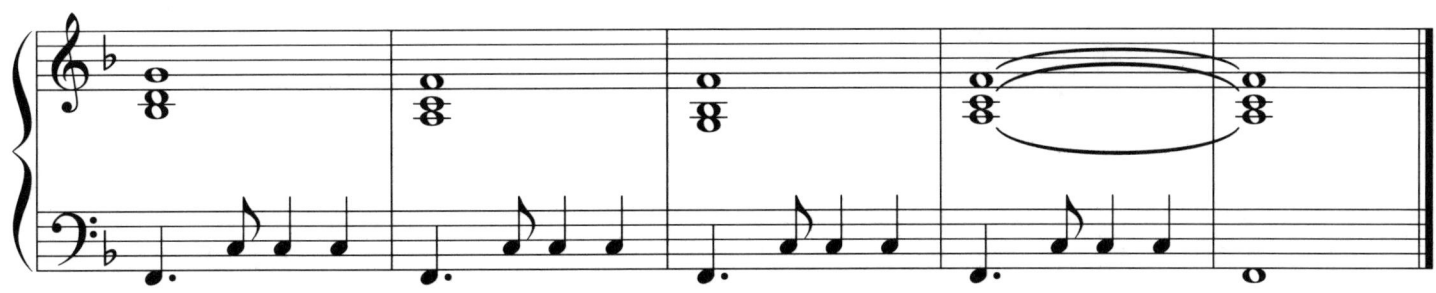

DAY 5